GETTING AROUND IN MY TOWN

I0793796

TAKING A BUS

By Owen Hamlin

Consultant: Beth Gambro
Reading Specialist, Yorkville, Illinois

BEARPORT PUBLISHING

Minneapolis, Minnesota

Teaching Tips

Before Reading

- Look at the cover of the book. Discuss the picture and the title.
- Ask readers to brainstorm a list of what they already know about taking the bus. What can they expect to see in the book?
- Go on a picture walk, looking through the pictures to discuss vocabulary and make predictions about the text.

During Reading

- Read for purpose. Encourage readers to think about the kinds of ways they can get around in their town.
- Ask readers to look for the details of the book. What are the steps to taking the bus?
- If readers encounter an unknown word, ask them to look at the sounds in the word. Then, ask them to look at the rest of the page. Are there any clues to help them understand?

After Reading

- Encourage readers to pick a buddy and reread the book together.
- Ask readers to name two things they might do while taking the bus. Find the pages that tell about these things.
- Ask readers to write or draw something they learned about taking the bus.

Credits
Cover and title page, © aapsky/iStock; 3, © RedBarnStudio/iStock; 5, © Leonid Andronov/iStock; 7, © RgStudio/iStock; 9, © AndreyPopov/iStock and © Hispanolistic/iStock; 11, © FotografieLink/iStock; 13, © Tomasz Wozniak/Adobe Stock; 14–15, © Igor Barilo/iStock; 16, © doomu/Shutterstock; 17, © bagira22/iStock and © Drazen/Adobe Stock; 19, © Odua Images/Adobe Stock; 20, © tzahiV/iStock; 21, © serhiibobyk/Adobe Stock; 22, © Laser1987/iStock, © serjiob74/Adobe Stock, and © nadorozhna.uliana/Adobe Stock; 23TL, © grinvalds/iStock; 23TR, © Garrett/Adobe Stock; 23BL, © Khaligo/Adobe Stock; 23BR, © mrak_hr/iStock.

See BearportPublishing.com for our statement on Generative AI Usage.

Library of Congress Cataloging-in-Publication Data

Names: Hamlin, Owen, 2000- author.
Title: Taking a bus / by Owen Hamlin.
Description: Minneapolis, Minnesota : Bearport Publishing Company, [2025] |
Series: Getting around in my town | Includes bibliographical references
and index.
Identifiers: LCCN 2024024241 (print) | LCCN 2024024242 (ebook) | ISBN
9798892326278 (library binding) | ISBN 9798892327077 (paperback) | ISBN
9798892326674 (ebook)
Subjects: LCSH: Buses--Juvenile literature.
Classification: LCC HE5611 .H36 2025 (print) | LCC HE5611 (ebook) | DDC
388.3/4233--dc23/eng/20240628
LC record available at https://lccn.loc.gov/2024024241
LC ebook record available at https://lccn.loc.gov/2024024242

For more information, write to Bearport Publishing, 5357 Penn Avenue South, Minneapolis, MN 55419.

Contents

Zoom!

Today, we are going to the zoo.

But we do not have a car.

How will we get there?

Let's take a bus!

There are many buses in our town.

They go to different places.

Which one can get us to the zoo?

We look at a bus map on our phone.

We find which bus we need.

The map also shows us the bus stops.

We can get on at any of these places.

Mill Park
VICTORIA STATION
San Marco
12th Avenue
1st Avenue
ARENA
EAST QUARTER
42th st
Rd 245
Park Ave
7th Avenue
St 65
12th Avenue
1st Avenue
METROPOLITAN UNIVERSITY
Park Ave
Bv Avenue
21th st
St 73
4th Avenue
Rd 56
Central Gardens
Pd Avenue
St 95
202
St 112
202
CITY TOWER
Rd 579
Red Bank
COLIN CENTRAL

The bus comes at certain times.

We do not want to miss it.

So, we get to the stop early.

There is a **shelter** to wait under.

A shelter

Many buses come to the bus stop.

How do we know which one is ours?

Each bus has a big sign at the front.

Sign
489 TEMPLE CITY
Metro Rapid
7904

Here comes our bus!

We stand back to stay safe.

We wait for the bus to pull up.

Then, the driver opens the door.

We line up to get on.

The first person steps up.

They pay with an **app**.

When it is our turn, we use a bus **pass**.

BUS TICKET

We look for a seat.

There is one in the back.

When everyone is on, the bus goes.

Our stop is next.

We pull a **cord** to let the driver know.

Ding!

We made it to the zoo.

I love taking the bus.

Parts of a Bus

A bus gets us around our town. Let's look at its parts.

Glossary

app something on a phone that lets people do things

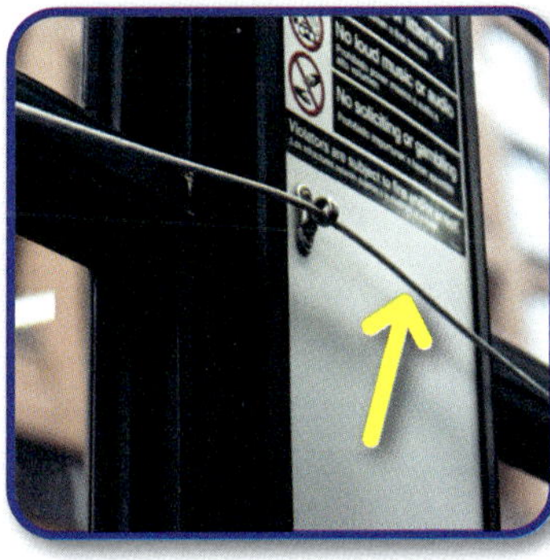

cord a piece of rope connected to something

pass a card or paper that is used to pay for things

shelter a place with a cover where one can stay safe

Index

Read More

Berne, Emma Carlson. *Transportation (Past and Present).* Minneapolis: Bearport Publishing Company, 2023.

Gates, Margo. *Wait, Ride, Walk (Pull Ahead Readers).* Minneapolis: Lerner Publications, 2021.

Learn More Online

1. Go to **FactSurfer.com** or scan the QR code below.
2. Enter "**Taking a Bus**" into the search box.
3. Click on the cover of this book to see a list of websites.

About the Author

Owen thinks taking the bus is great. He loves to do it when visiting cities!